# THE SPECTACULAR TRAINS

# THE SPECTACULAR TRAINS

## A History of Rail Transportation

Written and Illustrated by John Everds

DISCARD

Hubbard Press NORTHBROOK, ILLINOIS

# CONTENTS

CHAPTER ONE

# The Iron Horse Comes to America

Travel in early America changed very little from the time the first colonists arrived until about 200 years later. The earliest settlers were dependent on a few horses and mules and the wagons and buggies they put together themselves. Later, farmers used horses to pull wagons to transport produce to market or to take grain to the mill, to take families into town on Saturday or to church on Sunday. There were only a few narrow roads. In most places there were no roads at all.

To move heavy freight items, freight companies began building canals. It was easier to pull a load over a straight avenue of water than over a rutted, narrow road. Freight was moved much more efficiently this way. But no matter how good the canals were, goods and people could be moved no faster than the horses or mules that pulled them.

For many years, inventors had been experimenting with the steam engine. As early as 1705 Thomas Newcomen, a blacksmith from Dartmouth, England, built a stationary steam engine to pump water from coal mines. The Scottish engineer, James Watt, greatly improved on Newcomen's design in 1769. He fitted the engine with a cylinder and steam was injected into the cylinder to drive a wheel.

In the same year in France Captain Nicholas Cugnot constructed the first steam-powered vehicle to travel on land. His three-wheeled creation lacked brakes, however, and on its trial run in 1769 was demolished against a stone wall in Paris.

James Watt had a young assistant named William Murdock. Secretly, Murdock put together a steam-driven carriage in

1784, in a little village in Cornwall, England. He worked on the project secretly because Watt did not approve of using steam as a force to drive vehicles. So Murdock waited until late at night to try out his engine. But the three-wheeled machine got out of control and took off down the street without him. It hurtled past a church where the vicar, looking out the door, was certain that he had come face to face with Satan himself. The next morning Watt warned Murdock to stop experimenting with steam-driven vehicles at once.

Another English inventor, Richard Trevithick, produced the first steam locomotive to ride on rails. His locomotive *Newcastle*, built in 1805, was the first to have wheels flanged (or rimmed) on the inside to cling to the rails.

By this time steam was being used to propel river boats in America. In 1804 Oliver Evans built a vehicle that could run on land or water. Evans was commissioned by the City of Philadelphia to build a steam-powered dredging machine. He added four wheels to the dredge and drove it through the streets of Philadelphia. At the Schuylkill River it was successfully launched. This dredge, the *Orukter Amphibialis*, was the world's first self-propelled amphibious machine.

In 1825, one month before the Erie Canal opened, the first train powered by a steam locomotive was running on a public railroad in England. *Locomotion Number 1* pulled thirty cars down the tracks of the Stockton & Darlington Railway at the incredible speed of eight miles an hour. The "Iron Horse" had arrived.

In the same year an American industrialist built a small circular track on his property in Hoboken, New Jersey. For the entertainment of his guests, John Stevens constructed a locomotive that could pull a six-car train at speeds up to 12 miles an hour. This small locomotive, built in 1825, was the first to run on a track in America.

Most historians agree that the first American construction that could truly be called a railway was built by Gridley Bryant in 1826 to carry blocks of granite three miles from a quarry in Quincy, Massachusetts to Bunker Hill, where a monument was being erected. The cars ran on crude wooden rails and were pulled by horses.

Another three years went by before a locomotive operated on a public track in America. The Delaware and Hudson Canal Company operated a waterway from the Hudson River in New York to the Delaware River in Pennsylvania. In 1827 the company built a 16-mile railroad to connect their coal mines with the canal. At first, horses were used to haul the coal cars. But news of the successful use of steam locomotives in England prompted the canal company to send its promising young engineer, Horatio Allen, there to buy equipment. From the Foster, Rastrick & Company of Stourbridge he purchased four locomotives: the *Delaware*, the *Hudson*, the *America*, and the *Stourbridge Lion*.

The *Lion* was an impressive locomotive. It cost the canal company about $3,000. Its four large driving wheels were made of oak with iron tires, and the shiny black engine sported a gold and red lion's head on the front of its boiler. On May 15, 1829, the *Stourbridge Lion* was unloaded on the New York City docks. It was sent up the Hudson by riverboat and then by canal to Honesdale, where company officials were shocked to learn that the *Lion* weighed close to seven tons—four tons more than specified in the contract. This was a distressing situation, for on the trial run the *Lion* would be crossing a 30-foot-high wooden trestle that was built to support only three tons.

On the morning of August 8, 1829, against the advice of his friends and co-workers, Horatio Allen drove the huge beast over the swaying trestle and down the track for several miles before returning. Then and there it was decided that run would be the only one the *Stourbridge Lion* ever made. Seven tons of wood and metal was too much weight for flimsy tracks made of hemlock and capped by straps of iron. American rails were just not ready for the new steam engine.

9

Meanwhile, railroad builders in Baltimore were trying to work out a plan for horse-drawn trains. The Baltimore and Ohio Railroad planned to lay track from Baltimore to the Ohio River, using only horses to pull the trains along the 379 miles. The horses would be changed at 64 relay stations set up every six miles. The trains were to connect with the Chesapeake and Ohio Canal, but the plan was not a success. After only two years, the horse-drawn cars started to lose money. The railroad considered reducing service until a New York merchant came up with a plan.

Peter Cooper, a wealthy man, owned 3,000 acres of property along the Baltimore and Ohio right-of-way. Naturally, he wished to see the new railroad prosper. So he offered to design and build a new steam locomotive. The small machine he built could easily have been mistaken for a toy model. Peter Cooper appropriately named it *Tom Thumb*.

The *Tom Thumb* had only one cylinder, developing about one and a half horsepower. The boiler, about the size of a flour barrel, was mounted upright on a four-wheeled flatcar. Cooper, using whatever parts were handy, made boiler tubes out of gun barrels. The entire contraption weighed a little more than one ton and it looked, as one bystander remarked, "like a teakettle on wheels." On exhibition in 1830 the tiny engine, with Peter Cooper at the controls, pushed an open boat-shaped car filled with Baltimore and Ohio executives. It took the *Tom Thumb* an hour and 15 minutes to cover the 13-mile distance. At times the engine reached the great speed of 18 miles per hour.

On the return trip the driver of a horse-drawn car challenged Peter Cooper to a race. Cooper readily accepted the challenge and the race was on. As the little engine struggled to get up steam the horse galloped into the lead. Cooper threw more wood

10

on the fire. Gradually the pressure built up in the boiler and the *Tom Thumb*, puffing great clouds of black smoke, came charging from behind. The locomotive soon overtook the horse car, but the fan belt that operated the blower slipped off its pulley. The steam pressure dropped, *Tom Thumb* slowed to a halt, and the horse won the race.

Although the *Tom Thumb* was built as an experiment, it has the distinction of being the first locomotive built in the United States to pull a load of passengers over a public railroad.

In January, 1831, the Baltimore and Ohio Railroad directors held a contest. They offered a prize of $4,000 for the best coal-burning locomotive weighing less than three tons that could pull a 15-ton train 15 miles per hour. Out of the five entries, the engine judged best was the *York*, designed and built by Phineas Davis, a watchmaker from York, Pennsylvania. The *York* was put in service in July 1831 and Phineas Davis was hired as Baltimore and Ohio's chief engineer. The company continued to lay track westward and by 1834 the line had reached Harper's Ferry, West Virginia.

On Christmas Day 1830, the *Best Friend of Charleston* steamed out of Charleston, South Carolina. It pulled two wagons loaded with passengers. This was the beginning of regular rail service in America. This locomotive developed four times as much horsepower as Peter Cooper's *Tom Thumb* and was considerably larger, weighing almost four tons. Pulling several coaches, it could reach a speed of 25 miles an hour. With its bottle-shaped boiler mounted upright over the rear set of driving wheels, the *Best Friend* always appeared to be running backward.

The *Best Friend of Charleston* put in six months of regular service. Then one hot day in June a fireman, irritated by the hissing sound of escaping steam, tied down the noisy safety valve. For a short time there was blissful silence. Then the boiler exploded and blasted the *Best Friend* and its fireman off the tracks.

In the meantime a second locomotive was delivered. The *West Point* bore a family resemblance to the *Best Friend* except that the boiler was horizontal. To protect the passengers from future boiler explosions, six bales of cotton were strapped to a barrier car that was attached between the tender and the passenger cars. No provision was made to protect the engineer and fireman.

During the next few years the South Carolina Canal and Railroad became the longest railroad in the world and ultimately became part of the Southern Railway system. The 136-mile line was opened to Hamburg, South Carolina on the Savannah River in 1833. During these first years of development both the Baltimore and Ohio and the Charleston and Hamburg railroads devoted some time to testing sail-cars and horse-treadmill cars. Like a tiny boat on wheels, a sail-car could skim over the tracks at 30 miles an hour with a strong wind at its back. But wind was the problem: a headwind would push the sail-car in the wrong direction and a crosswind could topple it from the tracks.

On a horse-treadmill car the horse, surrounded by passengers, was actually placed inside the car. The horse was made to walk an endless belt, or treadmill, that transmitted power to the wheels. One such car, the *Flying Dutchman*, made a short trip at the speed of 12 miles an hour carrying 12 passengers. Both forms of travel were soon discarded.

The railroad-building craze was spreading rapidly from state to state. In New York state the Mohawk and Hudson Railroad started operating on 16 miles of track between Albany and Schenectady. Its locomotive, *DeWitt Clinton*, named in honor of the governor of New York, was built by the West Point Foundry and delivered to the railroad in 1831. The *DeWitt Clinton* was a small locomotive, weighing about three and one-half tons. It was only 11 feet long and its four driving wheels were 48 inches high. The wheels were made of wood and capped with iron.

On its trial run, the *DeWitt Clinton* pulled three bright yellow wooden coaches in addition to a flat car containing water barrels and a cord of fire wood. The open-windowed yellow coaches, with doors on either side, looked a lot like stagecoaches. Six passengers sat inside and six were seated on the roof. The iron wheels were flanged to grip the rails and the coaches were joined together by 3-foot lengths of chain.

When all the passengers were on board the conductor signalled with a shrill blast on a tin horn, the engineer opened the throttle, and the little locomotive bounded ahead. As the slack was taken up between the links of chain, the first coach lurched forward, followed by the second, and the third. Beaver hats toppled and passengers were pitched from their seats. As the locomotive picked up speed, sparks, soot, and burning embers spewed from the tall smokestack and rained down on those fashionably-dressed passengers who were sitting on the roof.

For the next few miles the riders frantically slapped at their clothing to put out fires. When the train stopped abruptly to take on water the passengers were hurtled again from their seats in the opposite direction. The train crew ripped apart a farmer's wooden fence and wedged pieces of it between the coaches. They were now held rigidly apart and the ride was tolerable, although on the return trip smoke and burning embers still made the passengers very uncomfortable.

Like other locomotives of this period, the *DeWitt Clinton* had no cab to protect the engineer and fireman, no whistle or bell, and no headlight. These improvements were to come later. A replica of the *DeWitt Clinton* is on exhibit today at the Henry Ford Museum in Dearborn, Michigan.

# CHAPTER TWO

# Railroad Fever

The Iron Horse was made to order for this robust young nation, eager to explore its new frontiers and expand its trade. Even though canals were important for transporting passengers and freight, "railroad fever" was quickly spreading from New England to the Gulf of Mexico. In 1830 there were only three locomotives and 23 miles of track in the United States. Ten years later there were 590 locomotives and 2,818 miles of track. Many railroads were very short lines, connecting towns with waterways or leading from mines to the docks of a nearby canal.

By 1835 Boston had become the rail center of the United States. Three railroad lines fanned out from the city. One ran north for 26 miles to Lowell, Massachusetts. This was the beginning of the Boston and Main Railroad. One ran southwest 41 miles to Providence, Rhode Island, with steamboat connections to New York. The third headed west for 44 miles to Worcester, Massachusetts. This line connected with the Western Railroad and reached Albany, New York in 1841.

Philadelphia was another rail center. The Camden and Amboy Railroad, chartered in 1830, finished laying track between Philadelphia and New York in 1837. The Philadelphia, Germantown, and Norristown Railroad had six miles of track in operation by 1832 and the Philadelphia, Wilmington, and Baltimore Railroad, chartered in 1881, was going full steam by 1837. But the biggest engineering gamble and by far the most incredible railroad of all the early lines was the Allegheny Portage Railroad. Built in 1834, it stretched 395 miles from Philadelphia to Pittsburgh and was a hodgepodge of tracks, rivers, and canals. At one point along the route canal barges were actually carried in sections on flatcars over the mountains much as trucks are carried "piggyback" on our trains today. The combined train-canal boat trip took three and one-half days. This made the journey between Philadelphia and Pittsburgh 17 days shorter than the route of the plodding Conestoga wagon.

By 1840 a railroad line existed as far west as Illinois and short lines honeycombed the eastern states from Maine to Florida. In fact, there were only four states east of the Mississippi River that did not have at least a short railroad track or a locomotive by 1840.

The earliest railroad tracks in this country were made from straps of iron fastened to wooden rails. These rails were secured to stone blocks. The tracks were crude and often very dangerous, for the iron straps had a nasty habit of working loose, coiling upwards, and piercing the floor of a moving coach. These broken strips of twisting metal were known as "snakeheads."

This problem caused untold damage to freight cars and passenger cars alike, until Robert Stevens arrived at a solution in 1831. While on a trip, Stevens began to whittle a wooden model of a T-shaped rail. He was confident this rail could withstand all kinds of weather and could support an extremely heavy weight. In England he had iron rails rolled to his T-shaped specifications. The rails, laid for the Camden and Amboy, were mounted on wooden ties and fastened down with hookheaded iron spikes. The rails held up well, and although smaller and much lighter in weight, were very much like the steel rails in use today.

Another serious problem was the varying width between the rails, also known as the gauge. The gauge used was 4 feet, 8½ inches from rail to rail. This has become the standard gauge in use today. It is probably just a coincidence that it happens also to be the gauge used on the ancient Roman chariots. On the early railroads in America, however, there was no such thing as a standard gauge. The distance between rails varied widely from a little over 4 feet to 6 feet. The varying gauges made it impossible to switch coaches or freight cars from one railroad to another. Cargo had to be unloaded then loaded again on a freight car of another line.

President Lincoln helped determine a standard gauge when he set 4 feet, 8½ inches as the gauge for the proposed Transcontinental Railroad in 1862. In 1887 all broad-gauge railroads finally accepted this gauge as standard for the country.

16

ME.

VT.

N.H.

Erie Canal

N.Y.

Albany

Rondout

Buffalo

Honesdale

D & H Canal & Railway

WIS.

MICH.

MINN.

IOWA.

PA.

Cumberland

National Turnpike

Wheeling

Baltimore

ILL.

Columbus

Indianapolis

B & O Railroad

IND.

W. VA.

MO.

Vandalia

Danville

Blockhouse

VA.

KY.

Wilderness Road

N.C.

ARK.

TENN.

Roads, Railways
& Canals of
1830

S.C.

GA.

Charleston

MISS.

ALA.

South Carolina R·R·

LA.

FLA.

It was years before fences were built all along a railroad's right of way. Farm animals often wandered onto the tracks, and a cow or even a large pig could easily derail an early locomotive. Isaac Dripps, master mechanic for the Camden and Amboy Railroad, placed two pointed iron rods on the front of the English-built locomotive *John Bull* in 1833. But unfortunately the engine speared the cows. Next, Dripps tried attaching a crossbar. Finally he settled on a wedge-shaped leading truck, which is believed to be the first successful "cowcatcher" installed on a locomotive. Early engineers believed that a full-grown ox could be thrown 30 feet by a good cowcatcher.

The *John Bull* was in service for the Camden and Amboy Railroad for 35 years. It is the oldest locomotive still in existence in the United States and is now on permanent display in the Smithsonian Institution in Washington, D.C.

Matthias Baldwin, a Philadelphia watchmaker, saw the *John Bull* when it first arrived in America. Soon he built his own full-scale locomotive, *Old Ironsides,* for the Philadelphia, Germantown, and Norristown Railroad. This was the beginning, in 1832, of the largest single-plant producer of steam locomotives in the world. Over the years, the Baldwin Locomotive Works has built 59,000 steam locomotives.

Headlights were not used on early locomotives because trains didn't run at night. But as traffic grew heavier and more miles of track were laid, night travel became necessary. In 1832 Horatio Allen, who was then chief engineer of the Charleston and Hamburg line, placed two flatcars in front of a locomotive. On the first car he built a bonfire of pine knots on a bed of sand. On the second he placed a simple reflector made of polished sheet iron. The bonfire was not very effective in lighting up the track, but Allen is credited with producing the first headlight used on a locomotive.

Hand lanterns were tried in 1834 but they were not successful. One of the first true headlights was installed on a Boston and Worcester locomotive in 1840. It consisted of a whale-oil lamp encased in a metal box backed by a tin-plate reflector. By 1850 headlights of this type were common. During the late nineteenth century headlights became very ornate, supported by graceful brass scrollwork and sometimes reaching a height of three feet. The lights were gaily decorated on the sides with paintings of harps, portraits, or landscapes. In 1859 kerosene lamps were first used, then gaslights, and finally, in 1881, electric headlights were introduced.

As speeds of the locomotive increased, warning devices were needed. Two warning devices soon became standard equipment —the bell and the steam whistle. Bells were fairly common by 1840. The steam whistle is thought to have been used first in our country on the Susquehanna and Hicksville Railroad in 1836. Ohio's first locomotive, in 1837, equipped with a whistle. On the Mad River and Lake Erie Railroad, the locomotive was the *Sandusky*. In time the engineers developed a code of whistle signals. This enabled them to communicate with the crew and with other railroad personnel. Modern diesel locomotives use air horns.

At about the same time, in 1836, cabs were added to locomotives to give the engineer and fireman some protection from the weather. One of the first railroads to adopt the cab was the Utica and Schenectady in 1836.

For the next 70 years, passenger cars would be made of wood. Opened windows provided the only means of ventilation but they allowed dust, smoke, and soot to pour in. Travelers still sat on hard upright wooden benches, and during the cold winter months stoves that burned coal or wood furnished some heat. At night the coaches were lit by candles covered by glass shields at each end of the car. The railroads started using oil lamps in 1850 and gaslights ten years later. In 1882 electric lights were used for the first time in a passenger car on the Pennsylvania Railroad.

WHISTLE TALK

Each • means a short toot.
Each ▬ means a long toot.

|  |  |
|---|---|
| • | Apply brakes. Stop. |
| ▬ ▬ | Release brakes. Proceed. |
| ▬ • • • | Flagman go back and protect rear of train. |
| ▬ ▬ ▬ ▬ | Flagman return from west or south. |
| ▬ ▬ ▬ ▬ ▬ | Flagman return from east or north. |
| • • • ▬ | Protect front of train. |
| • • | Answer to any signal not otherwise provided for. |
| • • • | When standing, to back up. When running, to stop at next passenger station. |
| • • • • | Call for signals. |
| ▬ ▬ • ▬ | Approaching highway crossing at grade. |
| ▬ | Approaching stations, junctions, and railroad crossings. |
| ▬ ▬ • | Approaching meeting or waiting points of trains. |

A number of short toots is an alarm for persons or livestock on the track.

19

Sparks pouring from wood-burning locomotives continued to plague the railroads. With the smokestack belching live embers nothing was spared. Passenger cars, baggage cars, freight cars, bridges, barns, woodlands—all were set ablaze. The railroads suffered vast property damage of their own stock and had to pay enormous claims to shippers when merchandise was destroyed.

In an effort to control the menacing sparks, builders gave smokestacks a variety of shapes, with names like Cabbage Head, Diamond, Balloon, and Sunflower. Wire screen bonnets were attached to the outside. Inside, inverted cones were used to deflect the sparks downward to collect in hoppers below. More than 1,000 patents were issued for smokestacks designed with some form of spark control, but the problem was never entirely solved until locomotives started burning coal.

Most of the early passenger cars were simply stagecoaches mounted on four flanged wheels. This is not surprising, because

Balloon

Cabbage Head

Diamond

Capstack

Sunflower

Straight

Modern

almost all of the body work was handcrafted by stagecoach
builders. One of the first departures in coach design was brought
about by Ross Winans, who was assistant to Phineas Davis at the
Baltimore and Ohio Railroad shops. To accommodate more passengers, Winans mounted three stagecoach bodies together on
one frame, supported at each end by a four-wheel swivel truck.
His first car, completed in 1831, seated 60 passengers and was
named *Columbus*. Later Winans designed a coach with a center
aisle with seats on both sides. By putting his car on springs he offered the passengers a softer ride. Freight cars developed more
slowly than passenger cars, and for a long time freight cars were
only primitive carts or wagons fitted to the rails. By the 1840s
swivel trucks were being used, although rigid four-wheel coal cars
or "jimmies" were used as late as 1880.

For many years every locomotive built in this country had
the wheels held in a rigid frame. This wheel arrangement worked
fairly well in England, where the railroads were generally
straight. But American railroads were uneven and full of curves.
Engineers had their hands full just keeping the locomotives on
the track.

Several developments greatly improved the handling of the locomotive. First, John B. Jervis, chief engineer of the Mohawk and Hudson, put four small wheels close together to form a truck and fastened it beneath the front end of a locomotive with a center pin. This allowed the truck to turn or swivel so that it could lead the engine over winding tracks. The swivel truck was first fitted to the locomotive *Brother Jonathan* in 1832.

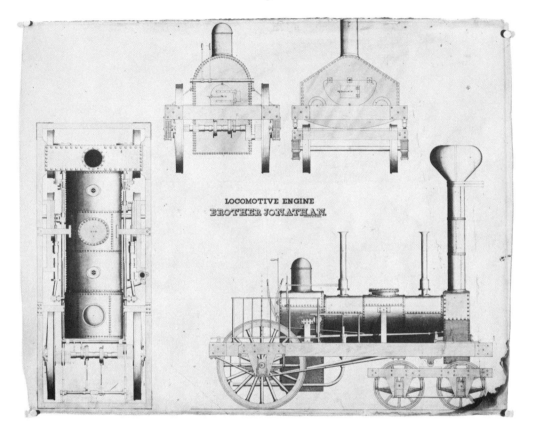

LOCOMOTIVE ENGINE
BROTHER JONATHAN.

The next step was to combine the swivel truck with four large driving wheels. Henry Campbell made the first major break with the English school when he designed such a locomotive in 1836. This type of locomotive, known as the American Type, had a four-wheel leading truck, four driving wheels, and no wheels behind the drivers. An engine with this wheel conformation is designated 4-4-0.

The American Type became a classic and was the most popular locomotive of the nineteenth century. Over 25,000 were built. Its popularity was due primarily to the fact that it was suited to all types of service, ran well over uneven tracks, and was inexpensive to build and maintain. The first American Type, the *Blackhawk*, was built by James Brooks in 1837. It could well be called the grandfather of all the steam locomotives that are running today.

The third step was the equalizing beam developed by Joseph Harrison in 1838. This beam distributed the weight of the locomotive evenly over the driving wheels, allowing the wheels to move up and down independently of each other and resulting in a more level ride. The beam was first applied to the locomotive *Hercules* on the Beaver Meadow Railroad.

As the railroads covered more and more area, the need for communication devices became more important, Samuel Morse was a portrait painter, but he was also an inventor who realized the importance of sending messages quickly. For many years he struggled to perfect an electrical device for sending and receiving messages. Congress finally approved the building of a telegraph line between Washington and Baltimore. On May 24, 1844, Morse tapped out the famous message "What hath God wrought?" The telegraph was an overnight success and within six years telegraph lines were to follow railroad routes as far west as Ohio.

But until 1850 the railroad rarely used the telegraph. Before that, when two trains were scheduled to meet on a single track, an agreement had to be reached in advance which train would wait on a side track for the other to pass. If one train was delayed the other train might be held up for hours. Or, the engineer might risk proceeding along the track until he saw the smoke of the other train. Then he could either back up or go ahead to the nearest siding.

One day in 1851 the New York & Erie superintendent was traveling on a westbound express. He had the good sense to telegraph ahead to see if the eastbound train had arrived at the next station, rather than have his train wait endlessly on a siding. When he learned that the eastbound train had not yet arrived, he sent the message: "Hold back eastbound train until further orders." But the engineer refused to move the train even under orders, so the superintendent himself took over the controls. He drove the train to the next station where the eastbound train was already waiting.

The directors were amazed by the time the railroad saved by sending the message by wire, and the New York & Erie started using Morse's invention all along the route. Soon engineers throughout the country were receiving their orders by telegraph. Today, traffic is directed smoothly over a vast system of intersecting communication lines and the whereabouts of every train is known.

23

CHAPTER THREE

# Railroad to the Pacific

On January 24, 1848, James Marshall was helping to construct a sawmill for John Sutter. He bent over to pick up some glittering nuggets along the south fork of the American River. He had discovered gold in northern California! As the news traveled back East thousands of adventurous souls left their jobs, their homes, and their farms and made their way westward to stake their claims. They all hoped to strike it rich. By 1849 the Gold Rush was in full swing. The peace treaty with Mexico had been signed, and California was now a U.S. territory, open for settlement.

To get to California, many of the Forty-Niners, as the gold seekers were called, traveled by boat 15,000 miles around Cape Horn. This voyage sometimes took from six to eight months. The most daring made a shorter trip across the Isthmus of Panama—a perilous 50 miles through steaming malaria-infested jungle. Many traveled overland on horseback, by stagecoach, or by covered wagon across dry plains, alkali deserts, and rugged mountains. The journey by covered wagon was as long as the boat trip around the Horn. For those who could afford it, the fastest way to travel was by overland stage, which covered the distance from St. Joseph, Missouri, to California in seventeen bumpy days. The railroads were no help to impatient prospectors, for there was not a single mile of track anywhere west of the Mississippi river.

But by this time, Ohio, Indiana, Michigan, and Kentucky all had short railroad lines. The *Pioneer,* the first locomotive in Illinois, made its initial run down the tracks of the Chicago and Galena Union, now the Chicago and North Western Railway, on October 25, 1848. The Illinois Central built its railroad with the

help of the first large federal land grant in 1850. By 1851 the Baltimore and Ohio Railroad had reached the Ohio River. That same year the New York Central, by connecting a chain of ten railroads, completed a route from New York City to Buffalo.

The *Pacific Number 3* is credited with being the first locomotive to turn its wheels west of the Mississippi. It made a five-mile run from St. Louis to Cheltenham, Missouri, on December 1, 1852. This was on the Pacific Railroad of Missouri, later to become the Missouri Pacific. The first railroad to reach the Mississippi from the East was the Chicago and Rock Island in 1854. The river was bridged two years later. By 1859 the banks of the Missouri River were reached by the tracks of the Hannibal and St. Joseph Railroad, now a part of the Burlington Northern.

In the decade from 1850 to 1860 railway mileage increased tremendously from 9,021 to 30,626 miles. Most of the network of rails was laid down in New England and the Midwest, with only 8,855 miles of track operating in the South. A plan was proposed to build a Pacific railroad from the Missouri River all the way to California. The railroad would be 1,776 miles long— more than twice as long as any railroad anywhere in the world at that time. Asa Whitney had proposed such a railroad and presented the plan to Congress in 1844, but with no success.

Theodore Judah also dreamed of a railroad to the Pacific. He went West to California in 1854 and built a railroad 21 miles long, from Sacramento to the gold mines in the Sierra Nevada foothills. A year later he was asked to survey a route over the mountains from California to the Nevada silver mines. On one of his surveying trips he came upon Emigrant Pass and Donner Pass, through which rugged mountain men and settlers had crossed the high mountains. These mountain passes provided a practical route across the High Sierras. From then on Judah devoted all his time to promoting a railroad that would link the eastern United States with the Pacific Coast.

Judah traveled twice to the nation's capital to put his proposal before Congress. Back in California he organized the Central Pacific Railroad, with the financial backing of four wealthy Sacramento merchants: Leland Stanford, a wholesale grocer; Charles Crocker, a drygoods merchant; and Mark Hopkins and Collis P. Huntington, partners in a hardware store. These merchants were soon to become known as the Big Four.

On his second trip to Washington, Judah aroused some interest. Civil War had been declared and the Union now saw the advantages of having strong ties with the West. President Lin-

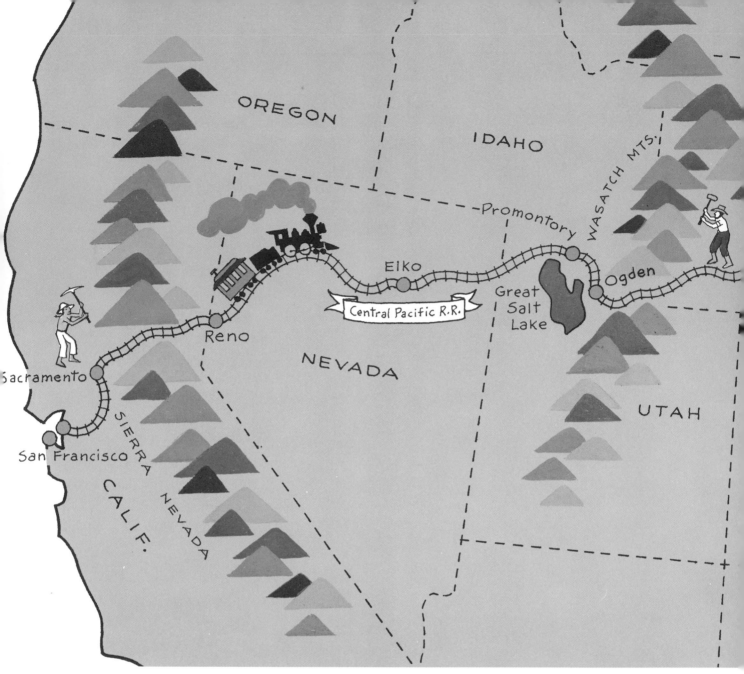

coln signed the Pacific Railroad Act authorizing two companies
to build a railroad and erect a telegraph line between Sacramento, California, and the Missouri River.

The Union Pacific was to start from Omaha, Nebraska, and
build westward to the California line. The Central Pacific was to
build from Sacramento to the California-Nevada border.

The government agreed to lend money to the railroads for
every mile of road they built: $16,000 a mile over prairies and
deserts, $32,000 a mile in the foothills, and $48,000 a mile cross-
ing the mountains. In addition, each company would receive
large grants of land to help finance construction.

When Theodore Judah returned once again to Sacramento,
he found that he and his backers disagreed on how the railroad

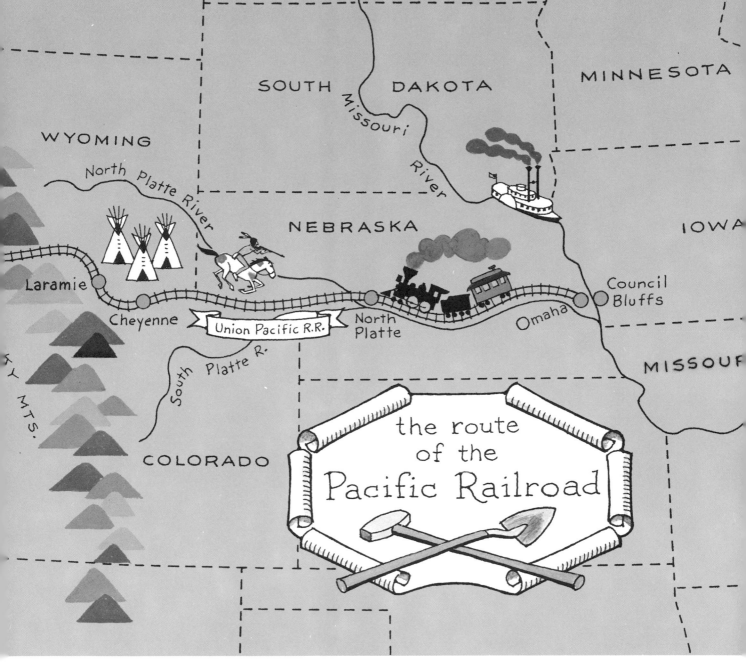

should be built. Judah believed it was worth the time and effort to have a well-built roadbed and properly laid tracks. His backers argued for cheaper construction and fast completion.

The Big Four finally bought Judah's interests for $100,000. They took control and proceeded to build the Central Pacific as swiftly as track could be laid. The Central Pacific broke ground in Sacramento in 1863 and by June of 1864 the track stretched to the foothills of the Sierras, 31 miles away.

The work was not proceeding on schedule because of two major problems: inability to transport supplies and lack of a labor force. Almost all of the building materials, including loco-motives, cars, and steel rails, had to be shipped from the East around Cape Horn. Only timber for railroad ties was abundant.

Tracklayers were especially scarce. Men were reluctant to sign on for such back-breaking work and, of the few that did, nearly half quit after about a week. In desperation Charlie Crocker, now in charge of construction, imported about 12,000 Chinese laborers to work for $35 a month.

The Chinese proved to be hard workers. Using only picks and shovels, mule-drawn dump carts, and black powder for blasting, the work crews hand-carved a roadbed through the High Sierras. At times it was necessary for Chinese workers to be lowered in wicker baskets over sheer cliffs to chip holes in the rock deep enough to plant black powder charges. After the fuses were lit, the baskets were quickly hauled up the face of the cliff as the explosions echoed in the canyon below. It was slow, dangerous work, but foot by foot the railroad tracks were spiked down.

In the spring of 1868, after digging 15 tunnels through solid granite and constructing miles of trestles over rivers and canyons, after climbing to a height of 7,000 feet while laying 125 miles of track, after battling storms that dumped 40 feet of snow on new roadbeds, after four years of this incredible effort, the Central Pacific finally reached the Truckee River on the Nevada border. The race across the Nevada desert had begun.

The Union Pacific broke ground in December 1863, but one year later no track had been laid. Tools, rails, ties, spikes, cars, engines, and provisions for the crew had to be shipped by river or hauled overland. Heavy locomotives had to be dismantled, placed in wagons, shipped to Omaha, unloaded, and put back together again. On top of that, there was a crippling labor shortage. But in 1865 the Civil War ended and the railroad finally began laying track. Thousands of former soldiers were hired. Among them was General Dodge, the new Chief Engineer hired by Union Pacific Vice President Durant. Wisely, he appointed two able brothers to take charge of construction. The rough and ready tracklayers became an efficient team.

The Casement brothers were probably the first to make use of the work train—a train that carried everything the crew needed. The first car carried the rails and spikes. It was followed by a carpenter's shop, a blacksmith car, a supply car, a telegraph car, a washhouse, a general store, a kitchen car, dining cars, several bunk cars, and perhaps a private parlor car. A herd of cattle driven alongside the train provided beef for the crew. The work train turned out to be a complete town on wheels. Near the close of 1866 the work crews reached North Platte, Nebraska—263 miles out of Omaha and averaging a mile of track a day. The route they followed was the Overland Trail, the one used by the Mormons and the Forty-Niners.

More obstacles were encountered as the railroad extended into Indian territory. At Plum Creek a party of Sioux warriors attacked a freight train, scalping the engineer and crew and making off with the provisions from overturned boxcars. General Dodge immediately armed groups of former soldiers to protect the trains. Again and again whole crews of workmen laid down their picks and shovels and grabbed Winchester repeating rifles to ward off Indian raiding parties. In the raids, telegraph lines were torn down, trains were burned, and hundreds of workers and Indians were killed. Still the railroad pushed westward.

In the meantime, the Central Pacific had very little trouble with the Indians. The railroad gave the chiefs of the Digger and Snake tribes free passes to ride the day coaches and let the braves ride the freight cars. No raiding parties were seen.

Late in the fall of 1867 the Union Pacific arrived in Cheyenne, Wyoming—493 miles from the Missouri river. The speed of laying tracks had increased from a mile a day to two, then three, then four. Soon the crews with their sledge hammers were spiking down as much as six miles a day. They took three strokes to a spike, ten spikes to a rail, and four hundred rails for every mile. Yet the ordeal was far from over. Ahead lay the Black Hills and the rugged Wasatch range of the Rockies.

Meanwhile, the Central Pacific was making up for lost time. By the end of 1868 track was laid halfway across Nevada on the Humboldt River. The Union Pacific was also drawing closer. The company had crossed the summit of the Rockies and by early winter was heading towards Ogden, Utah. In their speed the work crews sometimes laid rails on top of snow and ice-covered rivers. Once the tracks they put down on the bank of a frozen stream collapsed, and an entire train plunged into icy waters.

By Spring of 1869 the two railroads were approaching the northern end of the Great Salt Lake. Soon the locomotives were within whistling distance of each other. The rival companies continued to grade their roadbeds at breakneck speed. Word reached Charlie Crocker that early in April the Union Pacific had set a record of laying eight and a half miles of track in one day. Not to be outdone, Crocker bet $10,000 that his workers could lay 10 miles of track in a single day. The bet was covered by Union Pacific's Vice President Thomas Durant. On April 29, between dawn and dusk, Crocker's hand-picked crew did what people said was impossible. They laid 10 miles and 56 feet of track, a record that still stands.

The federal government was paying each railroad company $10,000 per mile of track laid. When they joined, no more income would come in. So both companies continued to lay track alongside each other for another hundred miles until President Grant insisted they agree on a meeting point.

The official site selected was Promontory, Utah. At noon on May 10, 1869, the tracks came together to join the Central Pacific and Union Pacific railroad. Two locomotives faced each other on the same track, the coal-burning Union Pacific *Number 119* and the wood-burning Central Pacific *Jupiter*. Between them a crowd of about 600 gathered where the rails would join.

The highlight of the celebration was the driving of the golden spike. A telegraph operator was standing by ready to broadcast the historic event to the nation. Leland Stanford, former governor of California and president of the Central Pacific, stepped forward, swung a silver sledge hammer—and missed the golden spike. He handed the hammer to Thomas Durant, Union Pacific's vice president, who took a hefty swing and also missed. The telegrapher took matters into his own hands and tapped out the one-word message, "DONE." President Grant received the message at the White House. The Liberty Bell rang out in Philadelphia, firebells rang in Chicago, New York City fired a 100-gun salute, and wild celebrations were set off all over the country. A construction superintendent drove home the golden spike without fanfare.

The Central Pacific had come 689 miles—the Union Pacific, 1,086 miles—to meet that day and to bind the nation together with a ribbon of steel.

32

# A
# PORTFOLIO
# OF
# TRAINS

1830

# Best Friend of Charleston

SOUTHERN RAILWAY

1837
# Lafayette
BALTIMORE & OHIO RAILROAD

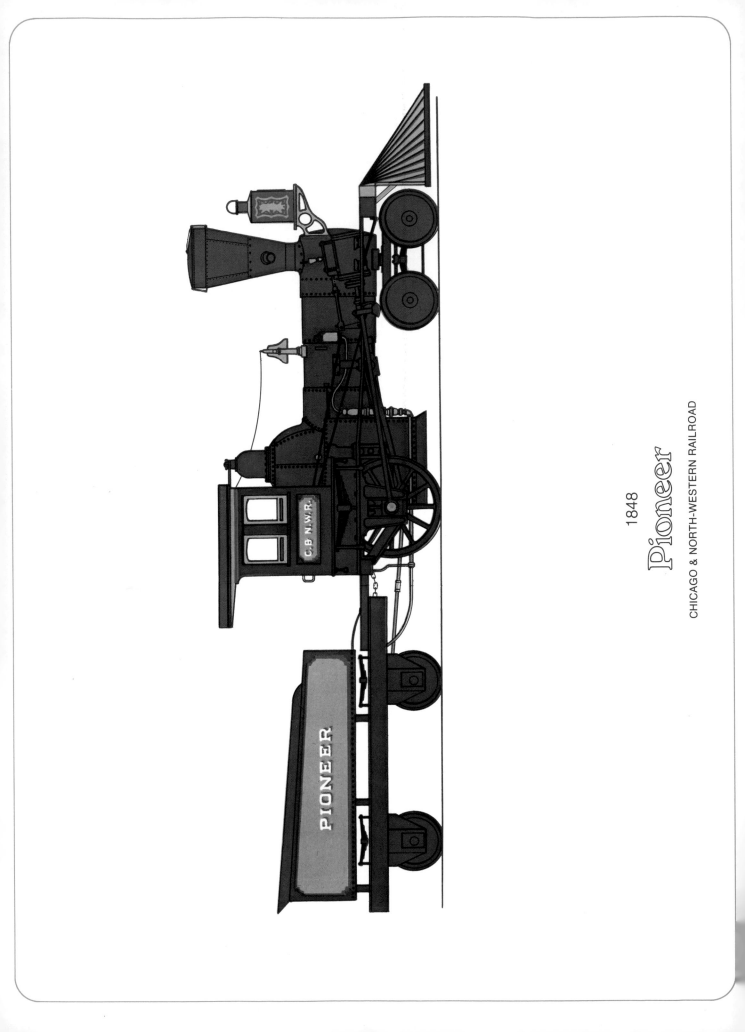

1848

*Pioneer*

CHICAGO & NORTH-WESTERN RAILROAD

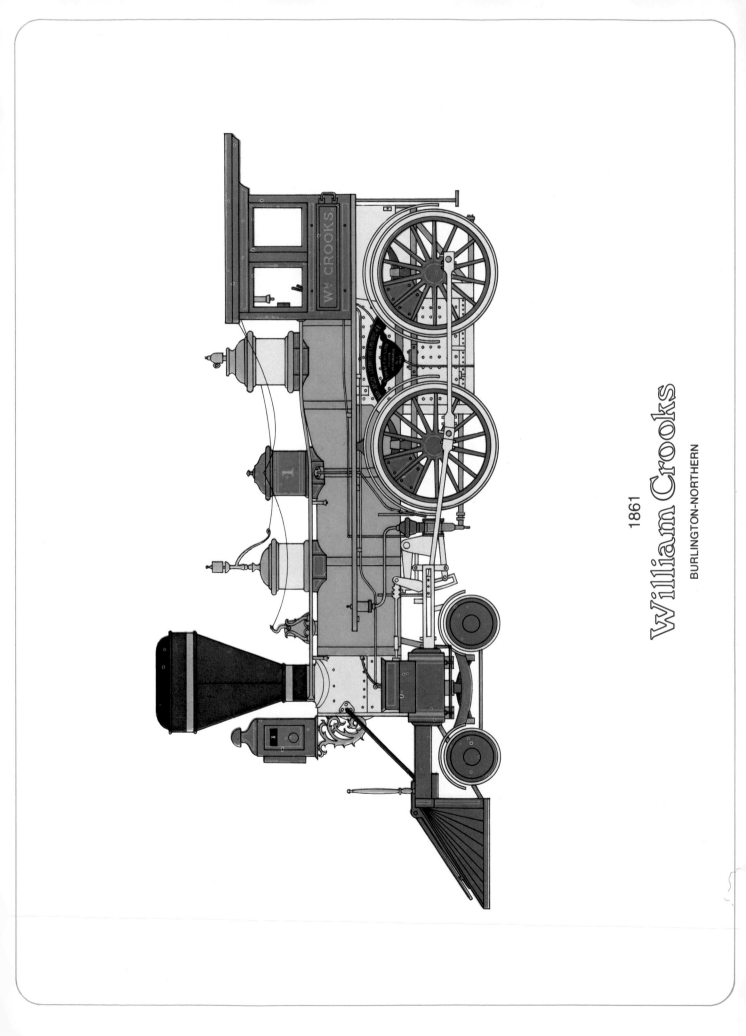

# William Crooks

## 1861

### BURLINGTON-NORTHERN

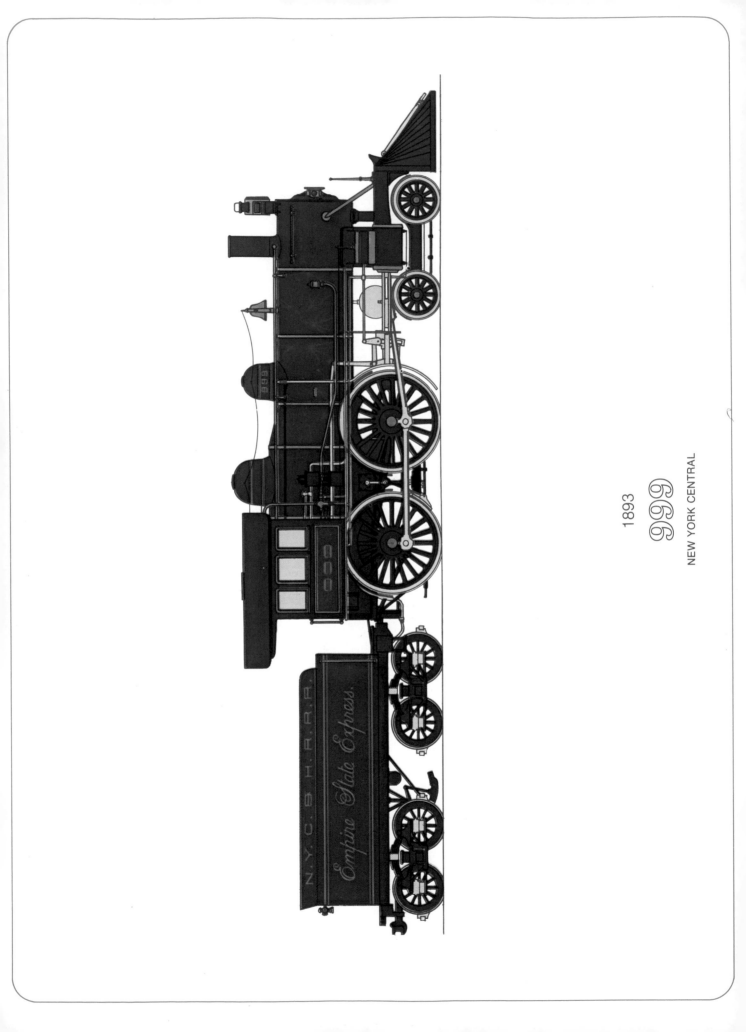

1893

999

NEW YORK CENTRAL

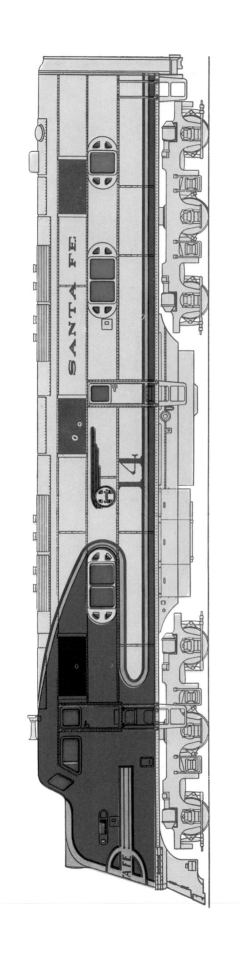

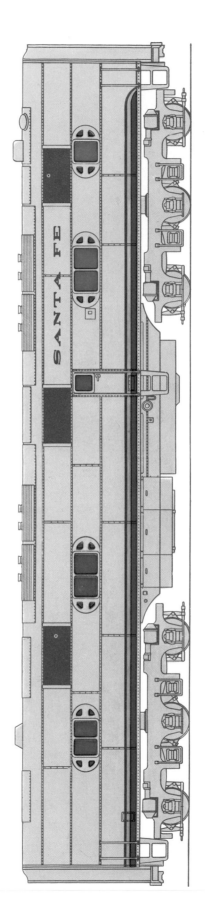

1939

"Super Chief"

SANTA FE RAILROAD

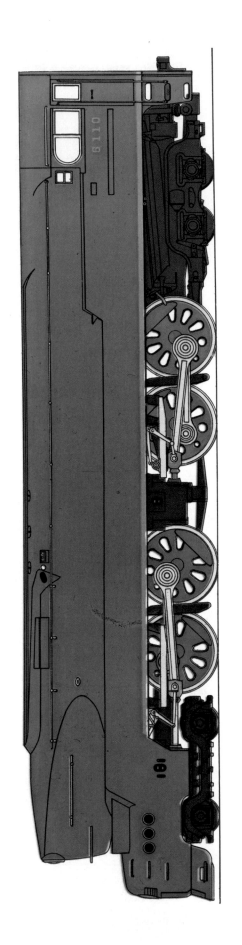

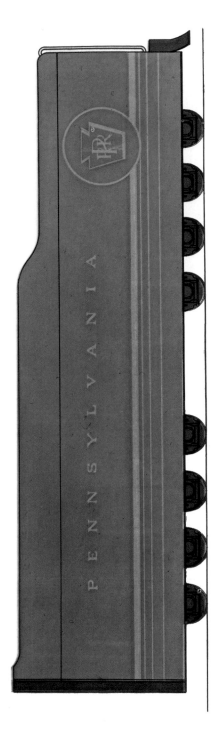

1942

# Admiral

PENNSYLVANIA RAILROAD

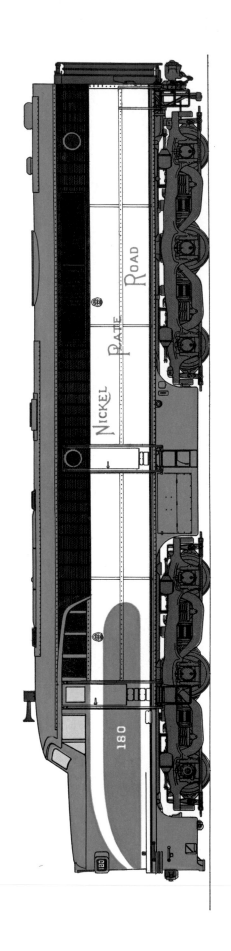

Alco PA

1946

NICKEL PLATE ROAD

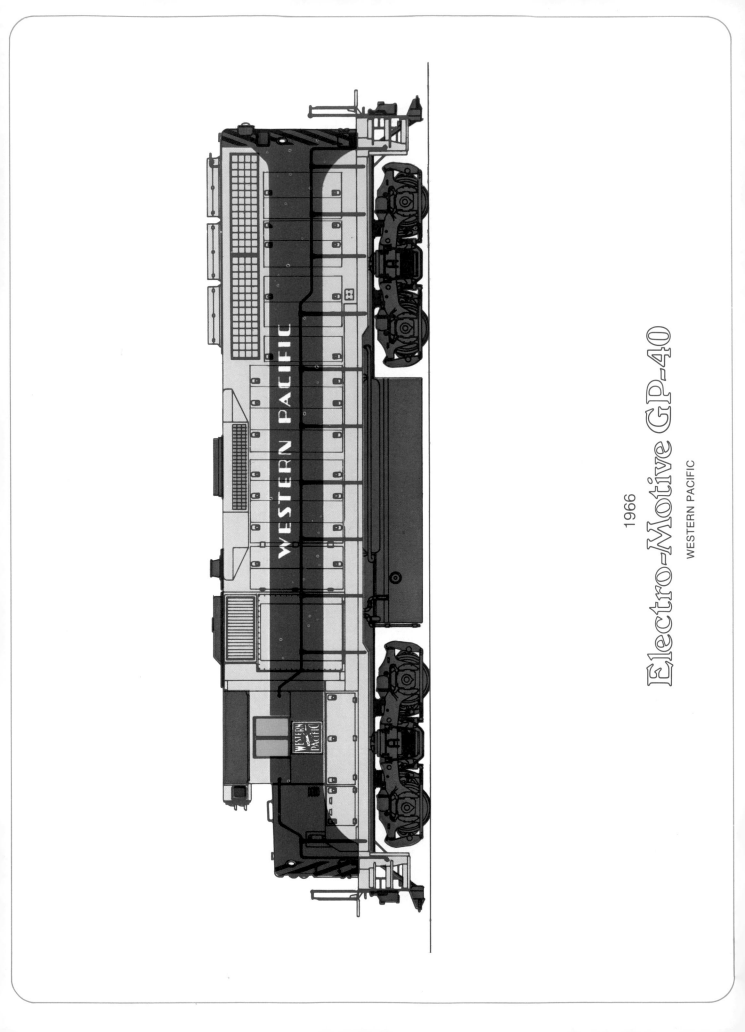

1966

# Electro-Motive GP-40

WESTERN PACIFIC

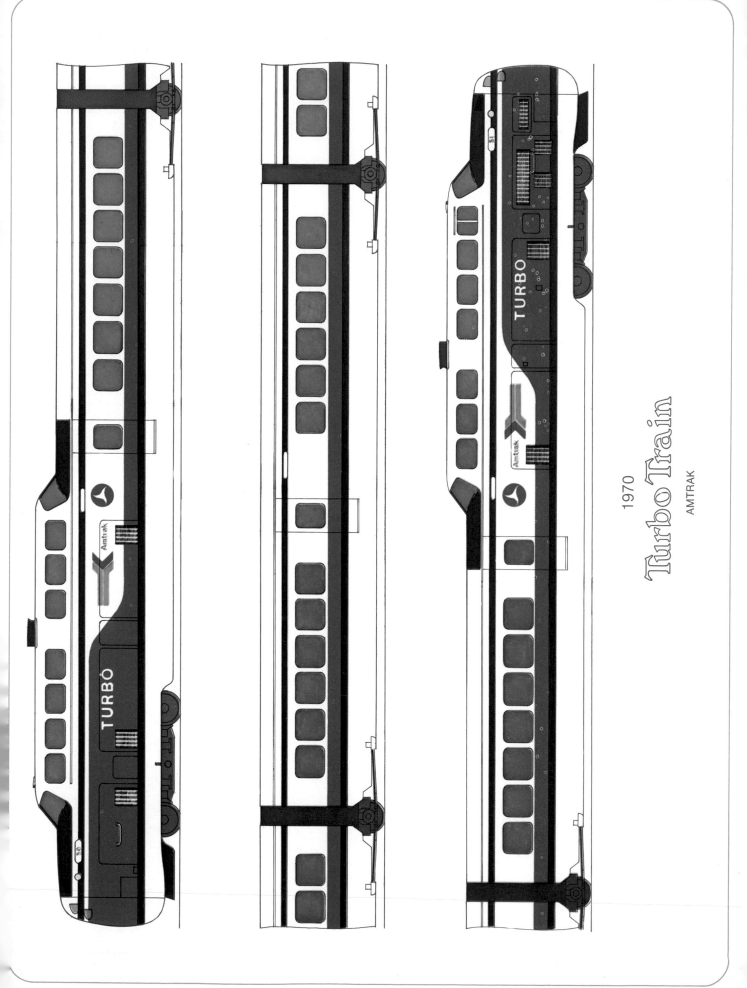

1970

Turbo Train

AMTRAK

# CHAPTER FOUR

# Gathering Speed

1 cowcatcher
2 leading truck wheels
3 cylinder
4 frame
5 steam chest
6 smoke box
7 headlight
8 smokestack
9 bell
10 sand box
11 boiler
12 steam dome
13 whistle
14 cab
15 driving wheels
16 fire box
17 eccentric rod
18 slide rod
19 pump
20 rocker arm
21 piston rod

Track mileage in this country more than tripled between 1850 and 1860, and the railroads greatly improved the technique of laying track. No longer were flimsy wood and strap iron used. The new tracks were laid on a roadbed of crushed rock using heavier all-iron T-rails. By 1865 steel rails were being rolled. By 1860, before the push to California, rails covered half of the continent, reaching westward into Texas, Louisiana, Arkansas, Missouri, and Iowa. The locomotive *William Crooks* pulled its first passenger train between St. Paul and Minneapolis in 1862. Chicago was replacing Boston as America's railway center.

The federal government continued its land-grant policy begun in 1850, to help construct new railroads. Congress would give a railroad alternate strips of land for six miles on either side of a proposed route, like the alternate squares on a checkerboard.

33

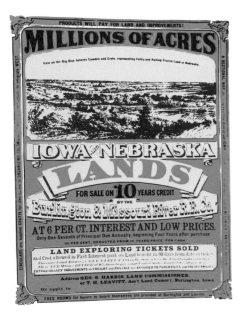

The railroad could sell or develop its land; the government offered the other sections to the public for $2.50 an acre. With the assurance of transportation and a market for their goods, the settlers eagerly grabbed the land. The West was ready to develop.

But in the years that followed 1850, the nation was painfully torn apart. In 1861 Civil War broke out between the states and all railroad development ground to a halt. The network of railroads in the North proved to be a great military asset to the Union cause. In 1862 the War Department organized a new branch known as the U.S. Military Railroads to bring together all the northern lines. The two biggest tasks assigned to the office were supplying the Union troops and transporting them.

No such organization existed in the South and the Confederates were never able to operate their railroads as a complete unit under one command. The South had less than half the track mileage of the North and it had fewer locomotives. Those that did exist had been built in northern foundries and shops, so the South had great difficulty repairing, rebuilding, or even maintaining a railroad. The rails themselves became a military target. Both sides were kept busy repairing tracks and trestles. Miles of track were ripped up by the opposing forces—the rails were heated and twisted around trees and telegraph poles.

But a major reason for the Union victory was the superior industrial and transportation organization in the North. The advantages of a nationwide transportation system became clear.

As the rail system grew, journeys were becoming longer, and people looked for more comfort on their railroad trips. Crude sleeping cars had been in operation as early as 1836 on the Cumberland Valley Railroad. These were simply small wooden coaches divided along one side into four sections, with three bunks, one above the other, in each section. The bunks, without springs, were nothing more than wooden shelves. The car was heated by wood-burning stoves and lighted by candles. Everyone brought his own blanket. Although it was called a sleeping car, it is hard to believe that any of the passengers spent a restful night.

George Pullman, a building contractor from Chicago, had traveled aboard a similar sleeping car when he was a young man. Pullman spent a sleepless night devising ways to improve the so-called sleeping car. In 1864, at a cost of $20,000, he built the *Pioneer,* the first fine Pullman car. The car was a foot wider and two and a half feet higher than the standard passenger coach. It was finished in handsome woods and luxurious upholstery with large washrooms. Every comfort was provided, including sheets and towels. But the *Pioneer* was much too wide to fit beside station platforms and too high to go through tunnels and bridges of that day. Pullman's sleeping car might have rusted away forgotten in some trainyard, except for one event.

President Lincoln was assassinated in 1865 and Mrs. Lincoln decided to have the *Pioneer* attached to the funeral train between Chicago and Springfield. So station platforms were shortened and tunnels were widened all along the route to accommodate George Pullman's creation. From then on the larger cars came into general use, and by the turn of the century Pullman owned and operated nearly all the sleeping cars in the country.

Although the Pullman Company also built dining cars, many trains, especially on the western routes, had no diners. The depot restaurants were invariably dirty and had a reputation for serving horrible food. A train would pull into a station for a 10-minute layover. Passengers would pile out and charge up to the counter for stale sandwiches and warmed-over coffee.

35

In 1876 Fred Harvey approached Charles Morse, the superintendent of the Santa Fe, with a plan. If the railroad would provide him with supplies and space he would open an eating house that would be a credit to the Santa Fe line. Fred Harvey was given a room at the Topeka, Kansas, depot. He scrubbed the room, repainted it, and added new tablecloths, napkins, and silver. He laid in a supply of good food and hired competent chefs. The lunchroom was an instant success. Soon Fred Harvey opened more eating houses, and they became famous because he offered elaborate dishes at low prices. A typical menu included pheasant, quail, golden plover or blue winged teal for one dollar. Venison was listed at 60 cents, sirloin steak was 50 cents, and lobster with broiled ham or bacon was only 40 cents. By the turn of the century Fred Harvey was operating 15 hotels, 47 restaurants, and 30 dining cars.

But Mr. Harvey is best remembered for his waitresses. In newspapers in the East and Midwest he advertised for "young women of good character, attractive and intelligent, between the ages of 18 and 30." Stress was placed on good character. The girls dressed in neat black uniforms with wide white collars and large white hair ribbons. At last the Wild West had a touch of grace and refinement. Although there was a rule that the girls couldn't marry for one year after seeking employment, it is estimated that more than 5,000 Harvey Girls found husbands among the engineers, conductors, brakemen, and station agents they met.

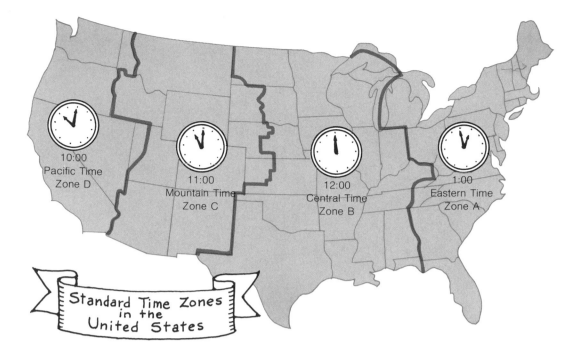

Standard Time Zones in the United States

Before 1883 there was no standard time. All the cities and villages throughout the United States were on "sun time." Clocks were set at 12:00 noon when the sun was directly overhead, but this time changed from city to city. When it was 12:00 noon in Washington, it was 12:07 in Philadelphia, 11:53 in Buffalo, 12:12 in New York and 12:24 in Boston. To make matters worse, each railroad could choose its own time. Trains pulling into the Pittsburgh terminal had their clocks set to six different times. In all, American railroads operated on more than sixty different times.

Railroad companies soon found that to operate efficiently, trains had to arrive and depart on time, locomotives had to be readied on time, trains had to be made up on time, baggage and mail had to be loaded on time, track repairs had to be finished on time, and train crews and station agents had to report on time.

Finally, in 1883, the nation was divided into four time zones. When it was 12:00 noon in the Eastern Time Zone, it was 11 o'clock in the Central Zone, 10 o'clock in the Mountain Zone and 9 in the Pacific Zone. It now became possible to publish an accurate schedule and with trains running on standard time many accidents were avoided.

Safety features were being developed, too, but some safety devices were a long time in coming. To replace the jolting chains that joined early carriages, a link and pin coupling was used. This was more comfortable for the passengers, but still dangerous for the crew. The brakeman, standing between the moving cars, had to guide the link into the socket. If he did not drop the pin into the link at precisely the right moment, the cars would come crashing together, causing serious injuries and many deaths.

37

Eli Janney, a major in the Confederate Army, patented a device in 1868 that he called a "knuckle coupler." Now when cars were pushed together they coupled automatically, like two hands gripping each other, and the brakeman could stand safely to one side and direct the operation. Present-day couplers are all patterned after the original Janney design.

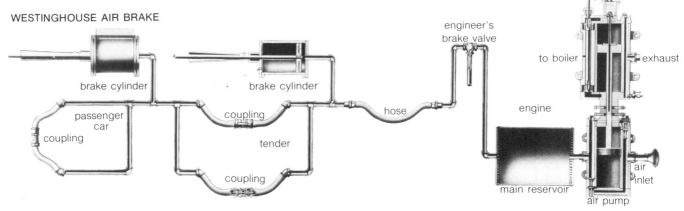

WESTINGHOUSE AIR BRAKE

Brakes were another problem. During the first decade of railroading, when a train approached a station the engineer would throw the locomotive into reverse. The driving wheels would spin and the engine would slide along the tracks. Quickly a gang of workmen would rush out, grab the locomotive, and try to bring it to a halt. Even though the train was proceeding slowly, this was a miserably inefficient way to stop.

Later, hand brakes were installed. When the engineer wanted to stop the train he gave a short blast on his whistle. The brakeman would dash madly from coach to coach setting the brakes, or stagger across the rooftops of swaying boxcars to twist the brake wheels. Often the train could not be stopped in time.

As a youth, George Westinghouse had witnessed a head-on collision of two trains in upstate New York. As he grew older he searched for a solution to the braking problem, and at the age of 22 he invented the air brake. He put an air pump and a compressed air reservoir on a locomotive. He ran air hoses from the air pump to the cars, connected to brake cylinders. When the engineer opened a valve air flowed through the hoses into the cylinders, setting the brakes. But there was one drawback: if there was a leak in the hose the brakes would not work. So Westinghouse reversed the system and air was forced into the hose live at a constant pressure to hold the brakes open. Now when the engineer wants to apply the brakes he lets air out of the hoses. Any major drop in air pressure will quickly stop the train. The air brake was a major contribution to railroad safety.

By 1880 railways existed in every state and territory in the United States. Almost 18,000 locomotives of one kind or another chugged along 93,000 miles of track. The following year the track mileage pushed past the 100,000 mark. 1881 saw the first passenger trains using steam heat in place of the hazardous coal-burning stoves. That year the Atcheson, Topeka, and Santa Fe reached from Kansas City to Deming, New Mexico, where it joined the Southern Pacific's route to San Francisco. This link formed the second line to the Pacific. The Southern Pacific extended its rails in January 1883 to New Orleans and in September the Northern Pacific was opened from St. Paul to Portland, Oregon. The Santa Fe completed its own line to California in 1888. Soon nine major routes connected the West Coast with the Midwest and the South.

The West was no longer a wild frontier. Population west of the Mississippi leaped from only 7 million in 1870 to 17 million in 1890. Cow towns and crossroads became thriving cities. Omaha's population soared from 16,000 to 140,000 and Denver's increased 20 times from 1870 to 1890. No single factor in history had so changed the face of America as the railroad had.

As the century drew to a close a new railroad speed record was set. For the first time a train traveled faster than 100 miles an hour. On May 10, 1893, on a straight run near Batavia, New York, Engine *Number 999* of the New York Central's *Empire State Express* reached the speed of 112.5 miles an hour, a record that was to stand for the next 12 years.

# CHAPTER FIVE

# The Golden Age

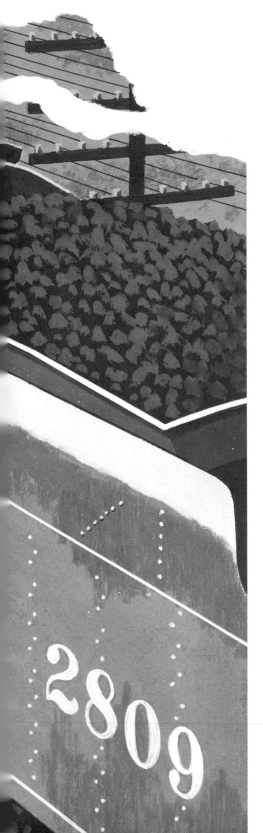

Railroading in America reached its peak during the first quarter of the twentieth century. New railroads were constructed on a spectacular scale. No longer was it always necessary to follow the contours of the land. Giant earth movers were used to produce an almost level roadbed with gentle curves across hills and valleys. The grade of a track is the rate of climb or descent. An absolutely level track has a zero grade. To keep the grade as close to zero as possible, builders used huge steam shovels, bulldozers, scrapers, and graders. Construction required enormous expenses. Still, by 1916 there were 254,000 miles of track in this country. Never again has so much track been in use. Nearly all the main lines had at least two parallel lines of track. Some companies had four parallel tracks to ease the traffic through congested areas.

Many of the gigantic passenger stations throughout the country were built before World War I. Some were built to look like Greek temples or Roman baths. The two largest were the Grand Central and the Pennsylvania stations in New York City.

Pennsylvania Station was built in 1910. Not too long ago when 950 trains passed through the station every day. The total building cost of the project was $115 million dollars. This included building and electrifying two tunnels leading into the terminal: one under the Hudson River to New Jersey, the other under the East River to Long Island. Modern air terminals must be built far outside the city limits, but the railroad depots were right in the heart of the cities.

Grand Central, completed in 1913, is the world's largest underground station. It covers 48 acres. The tracks are built on two

41

levels with 41 on the upper level and 39 on the lower level. At one time over 500 trains arrived and departed from Grand Central every day. This huge depot was a city in itself. Without leaving the terminal building, travelers had their choice of three hotels, many restaurants, varied stores, an art gallery, or movie theatres.

Chicago, the railroad capital of the nation, did not have the largest terminals but it certainly had the most. Seven passenger stations served 22 separate railroads. Recently several Chicago stations have been torn down to make way for other developments. Still, Chicago leads the country with 160 freight yards operating 7,720 miles of track.

Improved roadbeds and heavier, stronger rails could accept larger, more powerful locomotives. Locomotive shops added more driving wheels and larger boilers. They produced the Ten-Wheeler 4-6-0, the Twelve-Wheeler 4-8-0, and the Mastodon 4-10-0. These locomotives, generally used for hauling freight, were introduced before 1900. The Whyte system is used to identify these locomotives by their wheel arrangement. A Northern type, for example, has two pairs (4) of small wheels up front, four pairs (8) of driving wheels, and two pairs (4) of small wheels in the rear. The Northern, therefore, is identified as a 4-8-4 type of locomotive.

As the boilers grew in size, so did the fireboxes. To support this additional weight a two-wheel trailing truck was added. Locomotives with this wheel arrangement were the Atlantic 4-4-2,

42

built in 1894; the Columbia 2-4-2, built in 1895; and the Prairie 2-6-2, built in 1896. The Atlantic, with an increase in the size of its driving wheels, developed into a high-speed locomotive. It soon became a standard passenger type on many railroads.

The principal difference between a passenger and a freight locomotive was in the size of the driving wheels and the overall weight of the engine. Large driving wheels on the passenger types made greater speed possible. Adding more driving wheels of a smaller diameter gave a freight locomotive more traction. More locomotives with 2-wheel trailing trucks were the Mikado 2-8-2, 1897; the Pacific 4-6-2, 1901; and the Mountain type 4-8-2, 1912.

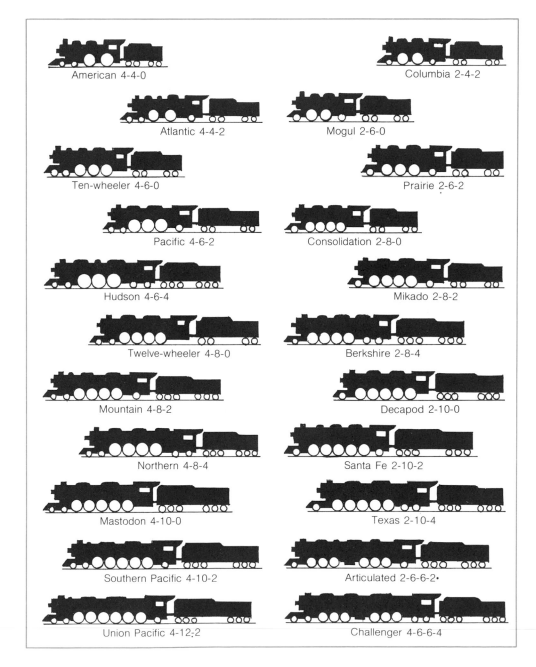

| | |
|---|---|
| American 4-4-0 | Columbia 2-4-2 |
| Atlantic 4-4-2 | Mogul 2-6-0 |
| Ten-wheeler 4-6-0 | Prairie 2-6-2 |
| Pacific 4-6-2 | Consolidation 2-8-0 |
| Hudson 4-6-4 | Mikado 2-8-2 |
| Twelve-wheeler 4-8-0 | Berkshire 2-8-4 |
| Mountain 4-8-2 | Decapod 2-10-0 |
| Northern 4-8-4 | Santa Fe 2-10-2 |
| Mastodon 4-10-0 | Texas 2-10-4 |
| Southern Pacific 4-10-2 | Articulated 2-6-6-2 |
| Union Pacific 4-12-2 | Challenger 4-6-6-4 |

The most powerful freight hauler to appear in the early 1900s was the Mallet locomotive, designed by Anatole Mallet, a French engineer. The Mallet might be called two locomotives in one. It had two engines and two sets of driving wheels under one boiler. They were joined together, or articulated, so that the huge locomotive could go around curves. The Mallet was in great demand for hauling heavy freight over steep mountain grades in the West and carrying coal over the Appalachians in the East.

By 1924 there were approximately 65,000 steam locomotives in existence. Since 1830 American shops have built about 180,000 locomotives. Most of these were produced by three companies: Baldwin, Alco, and Lima. Baldwin started building steam locomotives in 1831 and the company's output totalled 59,000. Nine companies combined in 1901 to form the American Locomotive Company, or Alco, which has produced 40,000 locomotives. Lima Locomotive Works, which started in 1879, has built 2,800 locomotives.

Before 1900 the speed of the average passenger train averaged about 35 miles an hour. There were exceptions: Engine Number 999, pulling the *Empire State Express,* set a record of over 100 miles an hour in 1893, and the Philadelphia and Reading Railroad had established a mile-a-minute schedule between Camden, N. J. and Atlantic City in 1897. But travel on most passenger trains was painfully slow until the New York Central put its *20th Century Limited* into service. It made a 20-hour run between New York and Chicago. The Pennsylvania Railroad matched that schedule with their *Pennsylvania Special,* the forerunner of the *Broadway Limited.* In 1905 they both reduced the time to 18 hours and soon the *Pennsylvania Special* set an unheard of speed record of 127.06 miles an hour.

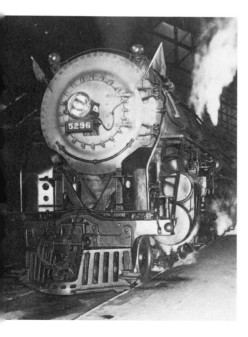

During the mid-1920s the steam locomotive was improved still further. To achieve higher speeds and more pulling power, the boiler and firebox were enlarged. But to do so without greatly increasing the existing wheel load required a redistribution of weight and the use of a 4-wheel trailing truck. Lima introduced the experimental A-1 in 1925, the first of the Super Power locomotives with a 4-wheel trailing truck. The A-1 had a 2-8-4 wheel arrangement, later referred to as a *Berkshire*. The next Super Power locomotive to make its appearance was the Texas 2-10-4. In 1927 the last of the Super Power locomotives appeared.

One was the *Northern,* a locomotive with a 4-8-4 wheel arrangement, designed primarily for heavy passenger duty. The *Northern* was a high point in locomotive development. More of these locomotives were bought than any of the other Super Power types.

The other was the *Hudson,* a 4-6-4 type that became the standard high-speed passenger locomotive of the New York Central. That railroad purchased 275 *Hudsons* in the eleven years they were being built. For over 20 years this reliable locomotive drove the luxury *20th Century Limited, Empire State Express,* and *Wolverine.* More than half of all the *Hudsons* built belong to the New York Central System.

Finally, with these new, high-speed engines, passenger traffic became both popular and profitable. It became very fashionable to travel across country on the fast, extra-fare luxury trains known as the *Limiteds.* Only the finest equipment was used on these magnificient trains, which consisted mainly of sleeping cars, diners, club cars, and sometimes open observation cars. The

### HOW A LOCOMOTIVE WORKS

Coal is fed through a conveyor trough (**a**) into the fire box (**b**). Flames and hot gases from the fire box heat water surrounding the boiler tubes (**c**) producing steam. The steam rises and collects in the steam dome (**d**). The engineer operating a throttle (**e**) lets steam into a large pipe (**f**). Steam passes into a steam chest (**g**) through valves into the engine's cylinders (**h**). Inside the cylinder a piston (**i**) is moved back and forth by the steam pressure. On one end of the piston is a connecting rod (**j**) which, along with a side rod (**k**), is attached to the driving wheels. As the piston moves, the connecting and side rods also move turning the driving wheels.
The spent steam passes into an exhaust pipe (**l**) which carries it into the smoke box and out the smoke stack (**m**) into open air.

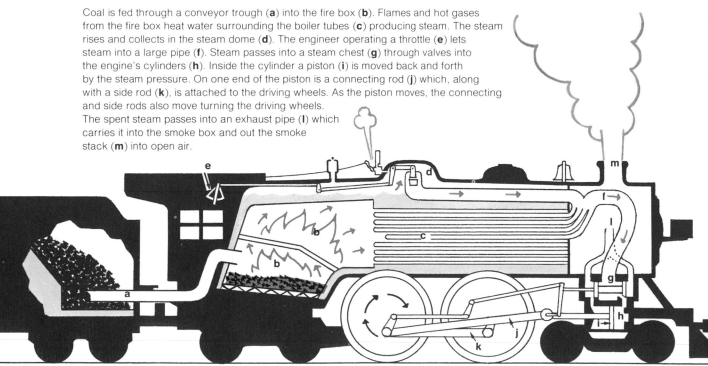

passenger's comfort was all important. Barbershops, baths, and valet service were provided, and maids, manicurists, and stenographers could be hired. Stock market reports and radio-telephone service were available to those who needed them. The *Limiteds* were also set apart from the other ordinary trains by the sumptuous food served on snowy-white tablecloths in the dining cars. Taking a trip between two major cities was like spending a night in a luxury hotel.

Almost every major railroad possessed at least one luxury train. The *Merchant Limited* operated between Boston and New York. This train, whose passengers were mostly bankers and stockbrokers, began in 1903 to make this trip in five hours. The famous *Capitol Limited* was the first all-pullman train traveling between Chicago, Washington, and Baltimore. A favorite of statesmen, ambassadors, and businessmen, it entered service in May, 1923. Its Washington terminus was Union Station just a few blocks from the major U.S. government buildings. In 1932 it became the first completely air-conditioned pullman train.

When the *Panama Limited* made its debut in 1911, the 921-mile trip from Chicago to New Orleans was made in 25 hours. In 1916 the *Limited* became an all-sleeping car train and the schedule was reduced to 23 hours. The time was cut to 18 hours behind a new diesel locomotive in 1942, and in the 1960s the *Panama Limited* was placed on a 16½ hour schedule.

In 1925 four railroad lines joined together to offer the finest travel accommodations ever between New York and New Orleans. A deluxe all-pullman train named the *Crescent Limited* maintained a 38-hour schedule traveling over the Pennsylvania Railroad, the Southern Railway, the West Point Route, and the Louisville and Nashville line.

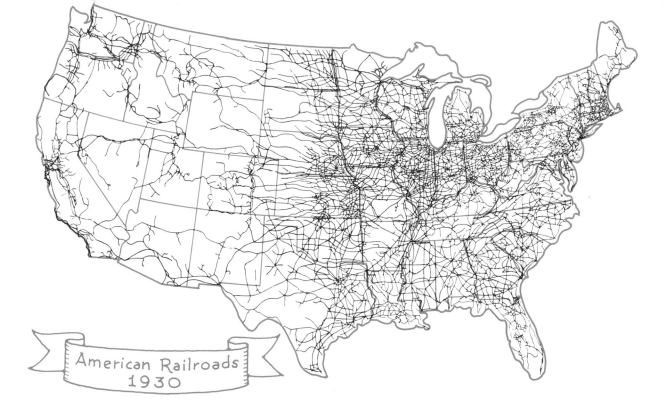

American Railroads
1930

Starting in 1896, the way to travel between Chicago and San Francisco was on the *Overland Limited*. Three major railroads cooperated to operate this train over their tracks. The 73-hour trip had shortened by 1930 to 56 hours. High-speed engines and track improvements made this possible.

For years the fastest and easiest way to travel was by train. No other form of transportation had emerged to seriously challenge the railroads. But after World War I, the American public fell in love with the automobile. Mass production had made it possible for many families to have their own cars. In the year 1920 almost 2 million passenger cars were built. The federal government began a highway building program and by 1927 Route 30, the Lincoln Highway, was completed. This 3,385-mile stretch of roadway joined Jersey City, N.J. to San Francisco, California. Intercity buses had been in operation in this country since 1914. By the time the Lincoln Highway was opened to traffic more than one million trucks were rumbling along the roads hauling freight from city to city.

As if this were not enough of a threat to the railroads, airlines started making transcontinental flights on a regular schedule in 1930, cutting days off a coast-to-coast trip by train.

The railroads seemed unconcerned by this competition. Although their passenger business fell off drastically, they did little to improve the quality of train travel until the high-speed, lightweight, air-conditioned streamliners were introduced in 1934.

# CHAPTER SIX

# The Age of the Streamliners

The revolutionary high-speed trains appeared in 1934 and captured the imagination of a country slowly emerging from the dark days of the depression. This was the year of twin-engined, all-metal, low-wing airliners, and of the "airflow" Chrysler and DeSoto automobiles. "Streamliner" was the latest word in our vocabulary. Streamlining is the styling of airplanes, automobiles, trains, and other vehicles so that they offer as little resistance as possible to the airstream at high speeds.

The first major streamlined train was the Union Pacific M-10000, later known as the *City of Salina*. The shape was tested in a wind tunnel. It looked a lot like a huge, glossy, brown and yellow caterpillar with a turret-like cab for a head. It was three feet lower than an ordinary train and about 200 feet long. It consisted of only three cars: a combined motor, Railway Post Office, and baggage car; a passenger coach with reclining seats for 60 people; and a second coach seating 56 people with a buffet kitchen tucked away in the tail. Built by the Pullman Company, the air-conditioned M-10000 was made of an aluminum alloy and weighed only 85 tons—less than the weight of a single standard Pullman car. In place of steam power, the M-10000 used a 12-cylinder, 600-horsepower Electro-Motive engine fueled by nonexplosive distillate of petroleum. In tests the lightweight streamliner reached speeds of 110 miles an hour.

In 1935 the M-10000 was put into regular daily service between Kansas City, Missouri and Salina, Kansas, making one round trip per day. This was an articulated train, which means that the cars were not separated, but joined together with only one truck beneath every two cars. This structure gave the train a smooth, unbroken surface from end to end.

The second streamliner was the *Burlington Zephyr*, built by E. G. Budd Manufacturing Company of Philadelphia. In many ways the *Zephyr* resembled its rival. The three-car stainless steel train was articulated, had reclining seats, and was air-conditioned. However, it carried only 72 passengers, was under 200 feet long, and weighed just under 100 tons.

The big difference between the two trains was the engine. The *Zephyr* was powered by a diesel engine. This new engine, named after its designer, is an internal-combustion engine that has no spark plugs. Instead, the fuel is ignited by compressed air. When air is under 500 pounds of pressure per square inch, the temperature is so hot it ignites the oil that is used for fuel. The engine is connected to a generator that produces electric current, which in turn drives the traction motors attached to the wheels. The diesel that powered the Burlington *Zephyr* was a 600-horsepower, 2-cycle, 8-cylinder Winton (Electro-Motive) engine.

## HOW A DIESEL ENGINE WORKS

The diesel engine has a four-stroke cycle. In the intake stroke, the piston (**a**) moves down and the air comes through the open intake valve (**b**) into the cylinder (**c**). As the piston reaches the bottom of the cylinder the intake valve closes. In the compression stroke, the piston is forced up and compresses the air. The temperature of the compressed air reaches approximately 1,000°F. Both valves close so the compressed air cannot escape. In the power stroke, diesel oil (**d**) is sprayed into the heated compressed air. The air-oil mixture explodes, forcing the piston down the cylinder. The connecting rod (**e**) moves the crankshaft, converting the vertical motion to rotary motion in order to move wheels. In the exhaust stroke, a flywheel completes the turn of the crankshaft, moving the piston back up the cylinder. The exhaust valve (**f**) opens and the waste gases leave the cylinder. The cycle begins again. Pistons in other cylinders are operating at different strokes so that the cycle is continuous.

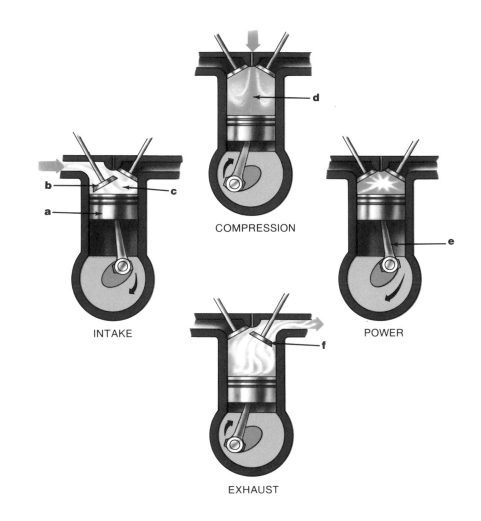

INTAKE

COMPRESSION

POWER

EXHAUST

For the first year the *Zephyr* was used more for exhibition than for carrying passengers. After a record-breaking, nonstop dash from Denver, the train arrived in Chicago to officially open the 1934 season of the "Century of Progress" Exposition. The 1,015-mile trip had taken 13 hours and 5 minutes. Later in the year, after a nationwide barnstorming tour and after playing the lead in the RKO movie "The Silver Streak," the *Zephyr* went into daily service between Lincoln, Nebraska, and Kansas City.

Then the Union Pacific launched the M-10001. This third streamliner set a new transcontinental speed record of 56 hours and 55 minutes. The six-car articulated train, later known as the *City of Portland,* had a 900-horsepower diesel engine. The immediate success of these three flashy trains set the stage for a colorful competition between diesels and steam.

The largest supplier of diesel engines was the Electro-Motive Corporation, a division of General Motors. Electro-Motive delivered the first streamlined diesel locomotive used in this country. It was the prototype for thousands of diesels yet to come.

Two Electro-Motive diesels were used in one of the most glamorous streamliners yet. A cab and a booster unit, together developing 3600 horsepower, pulled a striking bright yellow,

51

crimson, and silver train out of Dearborn station headed for Los Angeles. This was Santa Fe's *Super Chief,* the first diesel-powered all-Pullman train in America.

A favorite of movie stars and celebrities, the *Super Chief* symbolized the ultimate in rail travel. There were nine stainless steel nonarticulated cars: a Railway Post Office, a baggage car, 5 sleeping cars, a dining car, and a lounge car. The decorating scheme relied heavily on the Indian motif of the southwestern U.S. The plush *Super Chief* regularly made the 2,227-mile Chicago to Los Angeles run in less than 40 hours.

Another diesel supplier was Alco, the American Locomotive Company of New York, which had been a builder of steam locomotives since the 1850s. In 1940 the company merged with General Electric and began to build passenger diesels. Its most successful model, introduced in 1946, was a handsome passenger diesel with a cab slanted at a rakish angle and a long flat nose. The original model developed 2,000 horsepower from a 16-cylinder engine. Before production ended in 1953, 312 units were sold.

The next competitor was the Baldwin Locomotive Works, builder of the steam locomotive *Old Ironsides*. Its first diesel, built in 1925, was underpowered and was soon scrapped. Joined by Westinghouse in 1929, the company produced a variety of switching engines, but the most distinctive design by Baldwin was the "shark-nose" diesel, produced by Baldwin for the Pennsylvania Railroad in 1949. In the same year a 15,000-horsepower freight version was introduced, and close to 200 shark-nose diesels were produced in the next five years.

The Union Pacific placed orders for more diesels. The *City of Los Angeles,* the *City of San Francisco,* and two *City of Denver* trains were delivered in 1936. Burlington also put more *Zephyrs* into service. The *Twin Zephyrs,* running between Chicago and St. Paul, Minnesota, were followed by the *Mark Twain* and *Denver Zephyrs.* In 1935 the Boston and Maine Railroad began operating the *Flying Yankee* which was almost a carbon copy of the *Zephyr.* In Chicago, Pullman Standard delivered the *Green Diamond* to the Illinois Central. That train was built along the lines of the Union Pacific streamliner.

Not all of the railroads were eager to switch to diesels. Some companies decided instead to modernize their steam equipment. The New York Central led the way in 1934 with the Commodore Vanderbilt chosen to pull the luxury *20th Century Limited.* The Hudson-type locomotive was almost completely enclosed with a graceful metal covering, and finished in a gleaming gun-metal lacquer with silver trim. The effect was striking and also functional for the railroad claimed that at speeds of 70 miles an hour and more the shroud would reduce wind resistance by 35 percent.

For the streamliners, body styling was almost as important as speed, and the major manufacturers competed for the talents

of top industrial designers. The New York Central assigned designer Henry Dreyfuss in 1936 to dramatize its *Mercury*, a Pacific-type steam-powered locomotive, and in 1938 to modernize the *Hudsons* that moved the *Twentieth Century Limiteds*. Color and dash was brought back to the rails and the older-model steam locomotives were resplendent in hues not seen since the 1850s.

Raymond Loewy was an industrial designer who was much in demand. He styled the Pennsylvania Railroad's 1936 high-speed diesel, *Pacific*. The new streamliner headed up the company's crack express, the *Broadway Limited*.

Since World War II, handling freight has continued to be more profitable than hauling passengers. In the 1950s the railroads tried to inject new life into passenger service with an assortment of economical, ultra lightweight trains. The *Aerotrain*, which looked something like the old *City of Denver*, was the brainchild of General Motors. Built in 1956, it was made up of 10 bus-like cars carrying 40 passengers each. The weight of each coach was supported by eight bellows on an air-ride suspension system patented by General Motors. The engine, a V-12 diesel, delivered 1,200 horsepower. Two complete trains and a third locomotive were in use by the Rock Island Railroad until 1965.

The *Talgo*, based on a 1949 Spanish design, was called the most revolutionary train since the *Zephyr*. Built by the American Car and Foundry Company, the low-slung, articulated train had only two wheels per car. Each coach was only 9½ feet high, 4 feet lower than a standard coach, and only 20 feet long. The floor was a little more than 2 feet above the rails. The *Jet Rocket*, an ACF *Talgo* train, seating 300 passengers, was placed on the Rock Island's Chicago-Peoria run and pulled by an Electro-Motive *Aerotrain* engine.

The first electric locomotive to be streamlined was the Pennsylvania's GG-1. In the 1930s the Pennsylvania Railroad took on the ambitious project of completely electrifying many of its eastern main lines. The current was provided by overhead caternaries, or cables, that supplied 11,000 volts alternating current. Pennsylvania combined the various skills of Westinghouse and General Electric, Baldwin, and Raymond Loewy. The result was a brilliantly designed, high-speed passenger and freight locomotive, with 12 electric motors that developed 4,620 horsepower. It pulled heavy weights with ease. The first of these powerhouses went into service in April 1935. Many are still running today.

The last notable streamlined steam locomotive left the Baldwin shops in 1942 before the company became engaged in the war effort. Built for the Pennsylvania Railroad, the T-1 was unique in that it had four cylinders and four separate pairs of driving wheels in a 4-4-4-4 wheel arrangement. Another design from the drawing board of Raymond Loewy, its outstanding feature was the nose, which was shaped like a ship's prow. But this period of flashy styling provided only a short revival for the steam locomotive, which was fighting a losing battle with the diesel. No railroad company in America ordered a steam locomotive after 1952.

CHAPTER SEVEN

# Turbotrains to the Future

In the 1940s, immediately after World War II, passenger travel by rail became less and less popular every year. Most people found it quicker and more comfortable and convenient to travel by air. There were many reasons for this preference. The railroads were finding it more difficult to maintain luxury service on the crack long-distance trains. The government, which had given a great deal of financial aid to the railroads in their infancy, now was helping the airlines with money subsidies for passenger service development, airport building, and airmail handling.

The huge passenger stations, which were located for convenience in the downtown areas of cities, saw commercial areas crumbling around them, as business moved to the cleaner, roomier suburbs. After the war, cars became available, and fewer travelers used trains to get from city to city. The government also subsidized huge road-building projects, and driving became more convenient.

On top of all that, rising costs made it impossible for the railroad companies to make passenger transportation as profitable as freight moving was. As a consequence, even though the trains still moved passenger traffic, the people were neglected in favor of the freight.

It's no wonder that by 1970 the railroads were handling only a little more than seven percent of all the passenger travel in the United States, and there were less than 400 daily intercity passenger trains in existence, not counting regular short-run commuter trains. This is in contrast to the 1929 share of 77 percent of intercity travel on 20,000 clean, comfortable passenger trains.

57

Railroad and government officials had talked for more than ten years about a way of getting the railroad transportation business out of this slump, and of making trains more attractive to people. Finally, the Department of Transportation worked out a plan for government operation of passenger train service for an experimental period. The Rail Passenger Act became a law in 1970, and early in 1971 Amtrak was established. The board of directors was comprised of government and industry officials, and a basic system was mapped for the railroad network.

But what Amtrak took over was an old-fashioned business organization and run-down equipment. If changes were not made, Amtrak would lose more money than the railroad industry had lost, and no one would benefit. At first, many of the routes were cancelled outright, leaving some people who had suffered bad service with no service at all.

Reorganization was swift and complete, and by January 1973, 29 major routes were on the map, and 1,300 modern, or at least well-maintained, trains were in operation. More than 20,000 miles of track were in use, and 340 cities had trains stopping at their stations.

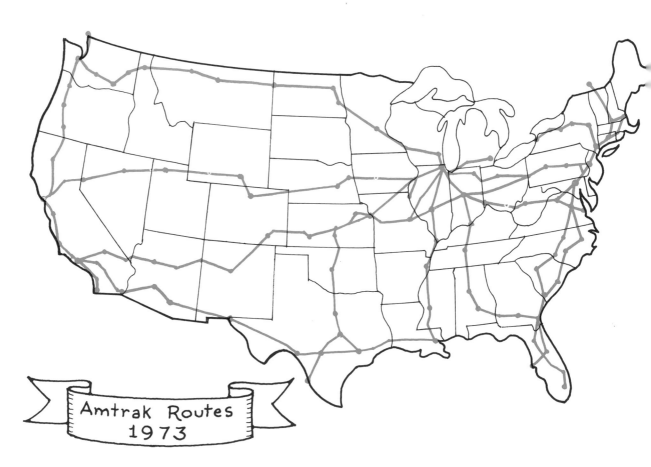

Amtrak Routes
1973

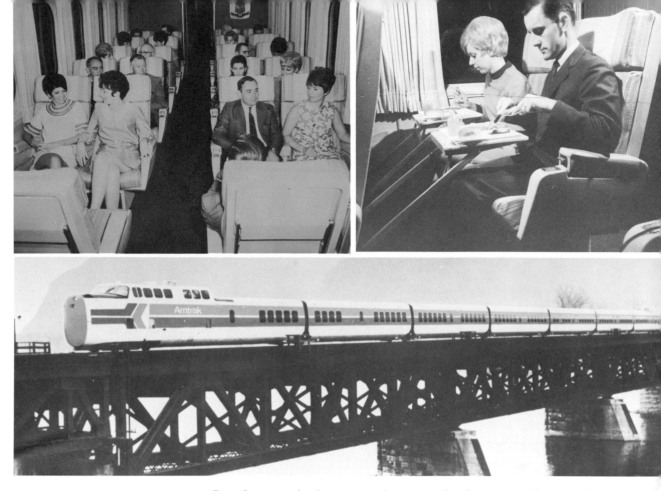

One feature the luxury trains never had, even in their golden age, was comfort for economy-class passengers. People who bought tickets for private rooms or even Pullman cars could travel in high-class luxury. They could eat in lavish dining cars on fine china and linens. But if you traveled by coach, you got an upright seat that did not recline, and you spent the long trip in that seat. For food, you had your choice of high-priced meals in the dining car or sandwiches brought from home. Amtrak is changing all that, with comfortable accommodations for lower-priced tickets, and a wide range of prices on food passengers can buy in snack-bar cars and lunch counters. Private rooms are still available, but they are smaller and less expensive than on earlier trains. More than twice as many of them are available in the same amount of space.

The new service is being effected without any new equipment purchases. The locomotives are of two types: *Metroliners* or *Turbo* trains. *Metroliners*, powered by electricity, run at high speeds but require overhead high-voltage electrical wiring for their power source. They are pollution-free. The Budd Company, an old name in locomotives, built them and leases them to Amtrak. They are in use for the eastern runs of intercity traffic, but not primarily for very-long-distance trips.

*Turbo* trains travel at a higher rate of speed (up to 172 miles per hour) and are in use on the cross-country schedules of the *Super Chief,* the *Zephyrs* to Denver and San Francisco, and the Broadway Limited. Turbos use the principles of a jet engine for their driving power. They are fueled by high-octane gas under pressure in a combustion engine. New models under consideration are capable of speeds up to 300 miles an hour.

Before these speeds will be safe, roadbeds must be improved. Seams where the rails join must be welded for extra strength, and the routes must be further leveled and straightened wherever possible.

Other modernizations are in line, too. These include expanded service and improvements in scheduling. For the first time, passenger train reservations and ticket sales will be plugged into a central computer terminal that will keep track of space available.

Amtrak has been given only two years to prove its worth, at which time Congress will review its performance and decide whether to continue the program, to advance more money, or to cut back on the funds allotted. Train travelers hope that the system will be able to show a profit and make coast-to-coast travel both possible and enjoyable again.

Amtrak **SOUTHWEST**

Amtrak...Takes You Clear Across America

## MAJOR EVENTS IN THE HISTORY OF RAILROADS

| | |
|---|---|
| **1705** | Thomas Newcomen builds stationary steam engine. |
| **1769** | James Watt improves on Newcomen's design. |
| | Captain Nicholas Cugnot constructs first steam-powered vehicle to travel on land. |
| **1784** | William Murdock builds a steam-driven carriage. |
| **1805** | Richard Trevithick builds locomotive *Newcastle*, first to have wheels flanged to cling to rails. |
| **1825** | First train powered by a steam locomotive runs on a public railroad in England. |
| | John Stevens builds a small locomotive that runs on a track. |
| **1826** | First railway built, in Massachusetts. |
| **1829** | Horatio Allen drives *Stourbridge Lion*. |
| **1830** | *Tom Thumb* exhibited; covers 13 miles in an hour and 15 minutes; races with horse-drawn car. |
| | On Christmas Day, *Best Friend of Charleston* leaves Charleston, S.C.; beginning of regular rail service in America. |
| **1831** | Baltimore and Ohio Railroad offers prize for best coal-burning locomotive; prize won by *York*. |
| | *DeWitt Clinton* completed. |
| | Robert Stevens invents iron rails. |
| **1832** | Horatio Allen produces first headlight. |
| **1836** | Steam whistle first used. |
| **1837** | First American Type locomotive built. |
| **1844** | Morse taps out first telegraph message. |
| **1848** | Gold discovered in California. |
| | *Pioneer*, first locomotive in Illinois, makes initial run. |
| **1850** | Federal government begins land-grant policy to help construct new railroads. |
| **1851** | New York & Erie Railroad first uses telegraph. |
| **1861** | Civil War breaks out. |
| **1862** | U.S. Military Railroads organized. |
| **1863** | Central Pacific and Union Pacific begin to build. |
| **1864** | George Pullman builds *Pioneer*, first Pullman car. |
| **1865** | *Pioneer* attached to Lincoln's funeral train. |
| **1869** | Central Pacific and Union Pacific meet to form first cross-country railroad. |
| | George Westinghouse patents his air brake. |

61

| 1876 | Fred Harvey begins railroad restaurant operations. |
|------|-----------------------------------------------------|
| 1881 | Passenger trains first use steam heat. |
| 1883 | Nation is divided into four time zones. |
| 1911 | *Panama Limited* makes its debut. |
| 1923 | *Capitol Limited* enters service. |
| 1925 | First Super Power locomotive introduced. |
| 1930 | Airlines begin making transcontinental flights on regular schedule; drastic effect on railroad passenger business. |
| 1934 | Burlington *Zephyr* opens Century of Progress Exposition. |
| 1935 | M-10000 (*City of Salina*), first major streamlined train, enters service.<br>First streamlined electric locomotive goes into service. |
| 1956 | *Aerotrain* and *Talgo* make their debut. |
| 1970 | Rail Passenger Act passed. |
| 1971 | Amtrak established. |

CREDITS

*Photo and illustration credits*
ACF Industries, pp. 46, 54.
Association of American Railroads, pp. 34, 38.
Baltimore and Ohio Railroad, p. 21.
Burlington-Northern, pp. 34, 35.
Chicago and Northwestern Railway, p. 26.
Chicago Sun-Times photo by Randy Leffingwell, p. 60.
Electro-Motive Division of General Motors Corp., p. 54.
Greenfield Village and Henry Ford Museum, p. 13.
Edwin Hough, p. 50.
Illinois Central Railroad, p. 53.
National Railroad Passenger Corp. (Amtrak), p. 59.
Norfolk and Western Railway, p. 37.
Pullman-Standard, p. 35.
Santa Fe Railway, p. 36.
Smithsonian Institution, pp. 8, 9, 16, 18, 22, 30.
Southern Pacific, pp. 26, 27, 31, 46.
Southern Railway, pp. 11, 12.
Union Pacific Railroad Company, pp. 32, 44, 52.
United States Information Agency, pp. 10, 38, 42, 44, 51, 52, 53, 55.

*Book design*
Willis Proudfoot

# INDEX